The Colors
We Eat

Sorting
Foods

Patricia Whitehouse

Heinemann Library
Chicago, Illinois

Customer Service 888-454-2279
Visit our website at www.heinemannlibrary.com

Designed by Sue Emerson, Heinemann Library
Printed and bound in the U.S.A. by Lake Book

06 05 04 03 02
10 9 8 7 6 5 4 3 2 1

Library of Congress Cataloging-in-Publication Data
Whitehouse, Patricia, 1958-
   Sorting foods / Patricia Whitehouse.
       p. cm. — (The colors we eat)
Includes index.
Summary: Introduces the concept of sorting using colorful foods.
   ISBN: 1-58810-539-3 (HC), 1-58810-747-7 (Pbk.)
   1. Food—Juvenile literature. 2. Color of food—Juvenile literature.
   [1. Food. 2. Color. 3. Set theory.] I. Title.
   TX355 .W48 2002
   641.3—dc21

                              2001004798

Acknowledgments
The author and publishers are grateful to the following for permission to reproduce copyright material:
pp. 3, 6, 7, 20, 21 Eric Anderson/Visuals Unlimited; pp. 4, 5, 8, 9, 10, 11, 12, 13, 14, 15, 16, 17, 22 Michael Brosilow/Heinemann Library; pp. 18, 19 Greg Beck/Fraser Photos

Cover photograph by Michael Brosilow/Heinemann Library

Every effort has been made to contact copyright holders of any material reproduced in this book. Any omissions will be rectified in subsequent printings if notice is given to the publisher.

Special thanks to our advisory panel for their help in the preparation of this book:
Eileen Day, Preschool Teacher
Chicago, IL

Paula Fischer, K–1 Teacher
Indianapolis, IN

Sandra Gilbert,
Library Media Specialist
Houston, TX

Angela Leeper,
Educational Consultant
North Carolina Department
of Public Instruction
Raleigh, NC

Pam McDonald, Reading Teacher
Winter Springs, FL

Melinda Murphy,
Library Media Specialist
Houston, TX

Helen Rosenberg, MLS
Chicago, IL

Anna Marie Varakin,
Reading Instructor
Western Maryland College

Some words are shown in bold, **like this.**
You can find them in the picture glossary on page 23.

Can You Find What Is Wrong?

Here are some foods, but something is wrong.

Some foods in these pictures don't belong.

What Doesn't Belong?

Here are some yellow foods, but something is wrong.

Which one of these foods doesn't belong?

The green **kiwi** doesn't belong.

What Doesn't Belong?

Here are some green foods, but something is wrong.

Which one of these foods doesn't belong?

The red tomato doesn't belong.

What Doesn't Belong?

Here are some red foods, but something is wrong.

Which one of these foods doesn't belong?

The white milk doesn't belong.

What Doesn't Belong?

Here's a white breakfast, but something is wrong.

Which one of these foods doesn't belong?

The red soup doesn't belong.

What Doesn't Belong?

Here's a red lunch, but something is wrong.

Which of these foods doesn't belong?

The yellow **pineapple** doesn't belong.

What Doesn't Belong?

Here's a yellow dinner, but something is wrong.

Which one of these foods doesn't belong?

The big green lettuce doesn't belong.

What Doesn't Belong?

Here are some big foods, but something is wrong.

Which of these foods don't belong?

The little red beans don't belong.

What Doesn't Belong?

Here are some small foods, but something is wrong.

Which one of these foods doesn't belong?

The big yellow banana
doesn't belong.

Here are the foods that
didn't belong.

This food is too good to last
very long!

What Belongs?

What should go in the red basket?

What should go in the green basket?

Look for the answers on page 24.

Picture Glossary

kiwi

page 5

pineapple

page 13

Note to Parents and Teachers

Reading for information is an important part of a child's literacy development. Using this book children can practice sorting by one characteristic, which is a basic mathematic skill. As you read *Sorting Foods* together, cover the photos on the right-hand pages. Ask children to identify the colors of all the foods on the left-hand page and predict which food is different. Then uncover the right-hand page to see if their predictions were correct. You can also play a sorting game. Place a row of like-colored objects, such as socks, blocks, or other toys on a table. Randomly place one or two objects of a different color in the row. Ask children to identify the objects that are the same, as well as those that are different. What are the differences? (These blocks are all green, but these are red.) Then ask children to make a group of objects for you to sort for a characteristic, such as color or shape.

Index

Answers to quiz on page 22

The red cabbages, red peppers, tomatoes, raspberries, red onions, pomegranates, strawberries, and radishes go in the red basket.

The zucchinis, green apples, green cabbages, green peppers, avocado, pears, and broccoli go in the green basket.